Original title:
Jewels in the Twilight

Copyright © 2025 Creative Arts Management OÜ
All rights reserved.

Author: Amelia Montgomery
ISBN HARDBACK: 978-1-80586-146-1
ISBN PAPERBACK: 978-1-80586-618-3

Whispers of the Night's Embers

As shadows dance like clumsy fools,
The moon trips over tiny stools.
A cat with style and sass galore,
Winks at the stars, then snores once more.

Fireflies buzz like talkative friends,
Their bright little stories, nobody lends.
They flash their secrets, then hide away,
Tickling the night before the break of day.

The Brightness of Silent Goodbyes

When the sun yawns and starts to fade,
The squirrels chirp like they just got paid.
With acorns stashed and pranks in mind,
They plot their spoils, oh how unkind!

A gentle breeze begins to tattle,
On the frogs who jump and start to rattle.
Each leap a plan, in the cooling air,
While crickets vote on who'll stay fair.

The Glint of Secrets and Stars

Stars gossip low in a sparkling choir,
While bats fly in like they own the shire.
With awkward flaps and a smirk so tight,
They claim the skies as their personal night.

The whispers blend with the hoot of an owl,
Who offers advice with a wise, soft growl.
But who would listen to such an old sage,
When the night is young and free from a cage?

Echoes of Dusk's Embrace

The twilight giggles as colors collide,
While ants march home, full of false pride.
With crumbs on their backs, they strut and parade,
Thinking their work deserves a grand trade.

As shadows stretch in a silly sway,
The dust bunnies gather for a colorful play.
Underneath the porch, they toss and tumble,
Amidst the leaves, they laugh and mumble.

Glimmers of a Fading Day

The sun slipped low, a giggling tease,
As shadows danced with the evening breeze.
A squirrel grinned, wearing a tiny hat,
While birds debated where to find a mat.

The colors swirled like a painter's dream,
Laughter rang out in the twilight stream.
A pair of frogs, so wise and spry,
Made croaky jokes that made me cry.

Twilight's Hidden Treasures

Underneath the stars, the puppies play,
Chasing their tails, a hilarious display.
A moonlit game of hide-and-seek,
Where every bumblebee starts to squeak.

A raccoon raids the picnic's delight,
Grabbing the last cupcake, what a sight!
With frosting smeared across his face,
He dashed away at a breakneck pace.

The Glow of Enchanted Nights

Fireflies blink like errant disco balls,
While cats plot sneaky, hilarious falls.
A star winks down, playing tricks on the owl,
As crickets chirp out a whimsical howl.

There's laughter in the air, no worries here,
As the moonlight spills like a fizzy beer.
The world wears a gown of quirky glow,
And everything silly just steals the show.

Celestial Luminescence

Planets twirl in a cosmic dance,
Where alien ducks seize every chance.
Wobbling through the galaxy's maze,
These quackers spark joy in a million ways.

A comet zooms for a grand old time,
While Saturn strikes a peculiar rhyme.
In this vast realm, giggles take flight,
As the universe redefines delight.

Echoes of Sparkling Dreams

In dreams so bright, they glow and gleam,
These little sparkles, how they beam!
Like fireflies in a silly dance,
They swirl around, all in a trance.

With giggles loud and ticklish feet,
They tumble, roll, and skip down the street.
A shimmering laugh escapes the night,
In every twinkle, pure delight.

Celestial Cascade at Dusk

As dusk arrives in playful haste,
Stars begin to flock with grace.
They tumble from the sky like rain,
Spilling laughter, joy, and gain.

The moon wears shades of purple hue,
While comets play a game or two.
With each bright flash, a silly joke,
A giggle fit, as stars invoke.

The Glimmering Cloak of Night

Tonight the night slips on its cloak,
With sparkles woven in with hope.
A sneaky wink from shadows deep,
As laughter stirs our dreams from sleep.

Beneath the stars, we dance around,
With silly hats and sounds profound.
Each twinkling light a jest or riddle,
In this bright game, we'll laugh and giggle.

Beneath a Canopy of Light

Under a blanket made of beams,
We frolic in a world of dreams.
Snickers echo, bright sparks fly,
While silly shadows leap and sigh.

A playful breeze whispers a tune,
As bright pinwheels spin 'neath the moon.
Each moment bursts with joyful cheer,
In this starry realm, we hold so dear.

Flickering Light Beneath the Stars

In the dark, the glow bugs dance,
It's a party of chance, oh what a prance.
Twinkle lights make the squirrels shine,
Who knew nature could host wine and dine?

The raccoons wear hats, oh, so fine,
Stealing snacks, sipping moonshine.
Crickets sing a silly tune,
As owls hoot, 'It's never too soon!'

Even the shadows hope to play,
Wishing they'd join in the buffet.
With giggles and chuckles, it's a sight,
Under the flickering light, pure delight!

Memories Wrapped in Night's Glow

The lanterns hang like old friends came,
Gossiping softly, sharing their fame.
Each flicker whispers a funny tale,
Of a cat on the roof, trying to sail.

As fireflies wink in a playful spree,
All the frogs croak, "Hey, look at me!"
They leap for joy, acting so spry,
Trying to catch a breeze passing by.

Old dog sleeps through the party fun,
Dreaming of chasing the moon, just one.
While the stars giggle, oh, what a show,
In the warmth of memories, wrapped in glow.

The Twilight of Fading Gleams

In the cozy dusk, shadows take shape,
A turtle in glasses decodes the tape.
Dancing leaves make a stampede sound,
As the flying tomatoes claim their ground.

The moon winks at the garden gnome,
Whistling songs from his little home.
A breeze teases, but oh, what a tease!
Flower pots laugh, swaying with ease.

As day drips away, echoes arise,
The sun waves goodbye with silly sighs.
With quirks and laughter, we cheer anew,
In twilight's embrace, where laughter grew.

Magic in the Evening Mist

With a sprinkle of mist, the fairies arrive,
On frogback scooters, they glide and jive.
They've lost their way in a marshmallow field,
Joking about wishes they forgot to yield.

Twirling in clouds, the sun's last rays,
Illuminate laughter that swirls and plays.
The wind tells secrets, oh, what a mix,
As owls drop puns with their wise-bird tricks.

Bumblebees buzz with a honeyed cheer,
Stumbling through daisies, spreading good cheer.
In the misty embrace, where giggles twist,
Magic awaits on the night's playful list.

Hues of a Mysterious Night

In the dark, squirrels wearing hats,
Dancing around like acrobats.
Moonbeams giggle, casting light,
Making chase with a cat in flight.

Flashing stars play peek-a-boo,
While owls hoot their silly woo.
Crickets chirp a merry song,
As shadows juggle all night long.

Luminous Echoes at Day's End

Fireflies flash like tiny cops,
Chasing the moon, oh how it hops!
A raccoon sneaks with a sly grin,
Stealing snacks from the trash bin.

The breeze tells jokes to the trees,
While night frogs croak in Tom and tease.
Stars trade stories, wild and bright,
As laughter spills into the night.

The Radiance of Evening Stars

Dandelions wear crowns of dew,
As ants march in a row, who knew?
The night's a stage, the crickets sing,
To constellations sharing bling.

Bats swoop low in an aerial dance,
Chasing shadows, taking a chance.
The moon winks, a cheeky sprite,
Inviting all to join the night.

Serenade of Shining Shadows

Giggling ghosts play hide and seek,
While the old, wise owl has a peek.
Rustling leaves share whispered jokes,
As the night air fills with hoaxes.

A wind-up cat spins on its tail,
Bouncing about without fail.
The stars roll laughter through the sky,
As evening stretches with a sigh.

Glimmers of Dusk

When evening comes with grins and chuckles,
The sun drops low, its light now buckles.
A squirrel dressed up in quite a flair,
Steals the last cookie, without a care.

The shadows dance in a wobbly way,
As birds discuss the events of the day.
A firefly buzzes, wearing a hat,
While frogs applaud, saying, "Dude, that's rad!"

Celestial Adornments

Stars hang like ornaments on a tree,
A cat struts by, pretending to be free.
With glints of mischief in moonlit pools,
The night wears an outfit that breaks all rules.

A comet zips past, quite out of breath,
While crickets stage a concert, full of zest.
The clouds giggle softly, not quite discrete,
As the Big Dipper can't find its seat.

Shadows of Sparkling Dreams

In the dark, dreams are wearing socks,
Chasing fireflies while playing with clocks.
A wise old owl wears glasses too small,
Says, "I see what I need, not much at all!"

A raccoon in shades finds shiny things,
While the moon plays tunes and softly sings.
Footprints in the grass lead to a chase,
We laugh 'til the dawn paints a new face.

Radiance Beneath the Stars

Under the twinkle, a rabbit hops,
Past shadows where the old lamp post stops.
Each ray of light, a tickle so bright,
Brings giggles to dance in the cool night.

The breeze whispers secrets to granola bars,
And ants put on shows, like tiny rock stars.
We wave to the clouds as they float on by,
Beneath the vast, outrageous night sky.

Glistening Veils of Evening

The moon sneezed softly, a twinkling sputter,
Stars giggled as they gathered in clutter.
A firefly wore shades, looking quite cool,
As crickets rehearsed for a nighttime school.

The cat wore a cape, a superhero vibe,
While shadows conspired to dance and imbibe.
A sprinkle of laughter lit up the sky,
With each twinkling star, a joke flying high.

Twilight's Secret Cache

In the twilight's purse, there's a sandwich unclaimed,
A treasure of pickles, though slightly inflamed.
The clouds play poker, betting on rays,
While the wind cracks jokes in a mischievous haze.

A sunbeam trips lightly on dew-slicked grass,
And whispers of secrets they'd share with the class.
The fireflies are giggling, drawing their maps,
As critters scurry home for their evening naps.

Reflections of a Dimming Sun

The sun wore a frown, its brightness on hold,
As shadows began to tell tales yet untold.
A squirrel, quite cheeky, stole some rays with glee,
While birds held a council, debating the tree.

The horizon chuckled, a soft brush of pink,
As stars played charades, leaning close to think.
With laughter erupting like bubbles in tea,
The day took a bow, as night yelled, "Yippee!"

The Silken Glow of Evening

The twilight wore laughter, draped in delight,
As bats flew past, giggling out of sight.
An owl cracked a pun, wisdom wrapped in fun,
While night's velvet cloak slowly came undone.

A comet buzzed by, in a flash, it said,
"I'll race you to stars, I'm the best at bed!"
The moon laughed so hard, it cracked a wide grin,
Inviting the night to let the fun begin.

Luster of the Vanishing Sun

As the sun slips behind the hill,
A hamster on a wheel keeps up the thrill.
The clouds are fluffing, like cotton candy,
While squirrels debate if they're too dandy.

With every wink from the evening light,
Crickets chirp jokes that take flight.
The sun makes faces, oh what a jest,
While shadows stretch, looking like guests.

The trees wear hats made of shimmering gleam,
Each bud winks like it's part of a dream.
As laughter echoes off leaves that sway,
The dusk holds secrets to laughter's play.

Glows of the Enchanted Hour

In the glow where mischief brews,
A cat on a skateboard gives bright views.
Fireflies giggle, flickering their grace,
While owls in glasses squint at the pace.

The moon's a pie, oddly placed on high,
Bats play tag with a cheeky sigh.
As frogs recite poems about their plight,
Laughter bubbles in the cool twilight.

With stars that twinkle in a silly dance,
Each one seems to have a secret chance.
They point and laugh at a nearby toad,
Whose hiccup echoes down the winding road.

Twinkling Echoes of the Night Sky

Underneath a cosmic blanket spread,
A raccoon juggles shiny marbles instead.
Stars giggle softly, like tiny lights,
As rabbits wear wigs for shenanigan nights.

Rover the dog barks a raucous tune,
While the moon takes selfies with a big spoon.
A comet zooms past, like it's on a quest,
Who knew the night sky could be so blessed?

Mice in tuxedos waltz on the lawn,
The breeze plays the harp, a whimsical dawn.
Each twinkling echo adds to the fun,
As everyone waits for the night's encore run.

The Dance of Dimming Radiance

As daylight bows to the vibrant night,
Belted owls wear ties, looking quite slight.
The moon gives a wink, and the stars reply,
With giggles that burst like popcorn on high.

Fireflies spark up a laughter parade,
While turtles in bowties feel quite displayed.
A melody flows from the bushes nearby,
As critters create their own joyful pie.

Each shadow stretches, ready to play,
With jokes in the breeze that skip and sway.
In this dance where radiance dims,
Laughter rings out, as the fun never swims.

Flickers of Twilight's Brilliance

In the sky's soft embrace, stars grin wide,
As critters dance 'round, their joy can't hide.
The moon's a cheeky chap, winks with delight,
While fireflies snicker, joining the night.

A cat on a fence stares, thinks it's a joke,
Chasing his shadow, he slips on the smoke.
The clouds wear pajamas, fluffy and bright,
Tickling the tips of games in the night.

Squirrels in sweaters tumble and slide,
While owls wear glasses, learning to bide.
Bats with their capes zoom past like a tease,
Who knew night's creatures could tickle with ease?

So raise a glass, let the laughter flow,
In this twilight hour, let silly things glow.
With nature's oddities prancing about,
The night's just starting, let's laugh and shout!

Nocturnal Lightplay

When dusk arrives, the raccoons prepare,
For scavenger hunts with a flair to share.
They've donned little hats, and oh, what a sight,
Raiding the bins, 'cause it's just their night!

In the distance, a croaking frog takes a bid,
Snapping his fingers to dance, that's his grid.
Fireflies join in, like a flashing parade,
While shadows behind them all nervously fade.

A dog walks by, thinks he's the queen's pup,
Chasing a squirrel who just won't give up.
In this frolicsome hour, with giggles all round,
Every nook and cranny holds laughter profound.

So come all ye dreamers, let's play this charade,
As stars twinkle brightly, and night masquerades.
In the silly schemes born when dark takes its throne,
We revel in antics, and all feel at home!

Gems of the Dusk

As sun kisses earth, a soft chuckle leaks,
The world transforms, and the humor peaks.
Crickets don tuxedos, ready to charm,
While bumblebees buzz with an airborne arm.

The clouds dress up in hues of delight,
Making puns in colors, a whimsical sight.
Squirrels toss acorns like jewels in flight,
Bringing laughter to every inch of the night.

The moon, a round joker, grins wide and clear,
While owls hoot jokes that only they hear.
Each shimmer and spark has a wisecrack to lend,
In the evening's glow where the laughter won't end.

So follow the giggles beneath the vast dome,
For in twilight's embrace, we're all free to roam.
With each sparkling glance, laughter takes flight,
In this merry ballet of creatures at night!

Luminous Whispers at Dusk

In a garden of giggles where shadows play,
The flowers burst forth with puns on display.
The daisies confide in the budding sweet pea,
Secrets of laughter, shared glee, and esprit.

With toads on a lily, there's ribbiting fun,
While frogs jest and leap, 'til the day is done.
The twilight spills stories, so bright and absurd,
As crickets recite the most comical word.

The fireflies buzz with a wink and a cheer,
Playing tag with the breeze, singing sweet and clear.
Only at night do they unleash their spree,
Twinkling like giggles, oh, what folly to see!

Embrace all the humor this dusk brings along,
In the glow of the night, let our hearts sing strong.
With each flicker and flutter, let merriment rise,
As laughter and light fill the vast, starry skies!

Twilight's Enchanted Traces

As the sun bids a cheeky adieu,
The moon plays peekaboo, too.
Stars twinkle like a disco ball,
Even the shadows start to sprawl.

Owls wear glasses, looking quite wise,
Raccoons in tuxedos stealing the skies.
Crickets chirp like a rock band show,
While fireflies dance, putting on a glow.

Mysterious Lustre of the Night

In the dark, a cupcake's a star,
Licked by a stray cat, how bizarre!
The clouds wear hats, oh what a sight,
While ants throw a party, out of delight.

Moonlight spills laughter on flower beds,
Squirrels juggle acorns, filling their heads.
It's a quirky gala, the critters unite,
In playful mischief, igniting the night.

Reflections of Midnight Magic

The clock chimes twice, causing a stir,
Rats in top hats begin to confer.
Mice waltz around, slick as can be,
Under a blanket of stars to see.

Candles flicker, making shadows dance,
While owls in bowties take a chance.
Balloons float by like giggling dreams,
In this nocturnal world, nothing is as it seems.

Glistening Veils of Shadows

Sneaky shadows slip on a cape,
Playing hide and seek - what a shape!
Luminous laughter tickles the air,
While bushes gossip without a care.

The crickets tap dance, what a delight,
Bats in shades zoom in with great might.
Each twinkle and shimmer, just for a while,
In this silly realm, let's stay and smile.

Enchanted Glimmer at Dusk

When the sky starts to wear a dark hat,
Fireflies giggle, a dance of the fat.
They twirl and they spin, not a care in their flight,
Count them if you can before they say goodnight.

A squirrel in a wig sneaks a peek from a tree,
He's plotting a sketch, oh what could it be?
A portrait of cats, with pride in their strut,
But he drops his paintbrush—oh, what a big nut!

The birds sing a tune that's terribly flat,
While turtles do yoga, a sight that falls flat.
Laughter erupts as they look quite absurd,
In this dusky retreat, joy sings without word.

So raise up a toast to the antics we see,
In the amber of dusk, wild and fancy-free.
With laughter as currency, we'll trade for the night,
For fun is the key to our shimmering light!

Enigma of the Dusk's Embers

In the twilight, a riddle that twinkles and beams,
The owls wear spectacles, or so it seems.
They hoot out equations like wise little profs,
Decipher this mystery, or are you just soft?

A raccoon's got tricks in his bandit-like paws,
He steals all the shine, and then he just guffaws.
"Who needs the moon?" he declares with a grin,
When the stars are all glittering, he wears a tin.

The shadows are sprites with a penchant for pranks,
They tease and they tickle the old wooden planks.
As laughter erupts in the soft silver mist,
We snicker at secrets that none can resist.

So toast with your friends to the whimsy and cheer,
In the enigma of dusk, we conquer our fear.
With silly old stories that wriggle and twist,
The night sparkles wildly, you won't want to miss!

Whispers of Light in the Gloom

In the night, whispers float like a soft pillow,
A cat in a cloak thinks he's quite the big fellow.
He struts through the garden, serenading the stars,
While the fireflies chuckle and giggle from afar.

The raccoons are wearing their finest tuxedo,
Performing a ballet with moves like a weirdo.
They twirl on the grass, with such comic finesse,
Who knew that the moonlight would make them confess?

"Can you catch a twinkle?" the shadows all ask,
As they hide behind stumps like a curious mask.
Laughter cascades from the trees overhead,
In this world of the wacky, hilarity's spread.

So gather your friends for this whimsical ride,
Where the whispers of twilight are giddy and wide.
With each little giggle, the gloom turns to cheer,
For in laughter and silliness, joy's always near!

A Dance of Fireflies and Fables

At dusk, the fireflies put on quite a show,
They twinkle and weave with a dazzling glow.
A frog joins the jig, with leaps that amaze,
While the crickets keep time in their rhythmic displays.

A rabbit in slippers hops in with a grin,
He's practicing ballet; just watch how he spins.
"Will you be my partner?" he asks with a spring,
The moon chuckles softly, oh the joy that he brings!

Each flicker a tale, spinning whispers of cheer,
As owls roll their eyes while drinking their beer.
"Let's toast to the magic of evenings so bright,
With laughter and fables to color the night."

So gather your dreams and your giggles galore,
For the dance of the dusk opens whimsical doors.
In the glow of the night, with friendship in play,
We giggle together 'til the dawn turns the day!

The Enigmatic Brilliance of Dusk

As the sun takes its leave, what a sight to behold,
Their sparkles of mischief, the stories retold.
Darkness creeping softly, like a cat on the prowl,
Whispers of laughter, the shadows all howl.

A squirrel in a top hat, a raccoon with a bow,
Shimmering secrets that only they know.
Twilight giggles and snickers, much to our delight,
The moon holds the punchline, with stars in a fight.

Fireflies flicker, like tiny disco balls,
Dancing with glee as night gently falls.
Each glance holds a chuckle, a wink from above,
In this whimsical realm, we find all the love.

Then comes a breeze with a playful embrace,
Tickling the leaves, putting smiles on each face.
In this puzzling hour, we all play the fool,
With a chuckle and shine, under night's golden rule.

Ethereal Dances in Darkened Air

Under the shroud of night's gentle sway,
A band of shadowy figures come out to play.
Moonlight's their spotlight, laughter their tune,
While crickets conduct a whimsical croon.

A fox in a tutu, prancing with flair,
While owls in tuxedos provide the night's air.
They twirl and they twist in a dazzling show,
With cheeky grins blinking, 'Where did time go?'

Even the stars seem to giggle and wink,
As fireflies join in, not missing a blink.
In the kaleidoscope sky, their pranks fill the night,
With colors and chaos, everything feels right.

Cheers rise from the grass, as marshmallows roast,
A raccoon's sly grin is what we love most.
In shadows, we find the humor and glee,
As night wraps its arms in a warm jubilee.

Hints of Light Between the Hours

As day slips away, and the night starts to creep,
Silly shadows awaken from their curious sleep.
Frogs don their slippers, and crickets tune up,
For the late-night dance party, grab your teacup.

A beetle with flair, on a leaf takes a stand,
While fireflies bring sparkles, like dust from a band.
In the twilight they boogie, with laughter they soar,
Who knew evening creatures could party like this more?

The air thick with giggles, like bubbles that pop,
As raccoons in glimmer, make sure to stop.
"Do you have the time?" asks a skunk in a tie,
While a raccoon replies, "It's 'whenever'," oh my!

So let's tiptoe softly through this fun-filled haze,
Where every shadow jigs in the twilight's gaze.
Hints of mischief and mirth grace the night,
With a wink from the stars, everything feels right.

The Soft Radiance of Evening

Evening rolls in with its clumsy parade,
Squirrels doing limbo, and raccoons invade.
With moonbeams as spotlights, they strut and they prance,
Making owls the judges at this merry dance.

The stars come in clusters, like friends at a bar,
Each twinkle a giggle, each blink is bizarre.
A bear in a bowtie, juggling pine cones,
While behind him, the hedgehogs share quirky tones.

As night paints with colors of super-fine gore,
Every laughter and shadow finds room to explore.
Mice wear tiny hats, as they sneak in a snack,
While fireflies laugh gently, lighting up the track.

Under the soft glow where the weirdos unite,
Evening's a party, so laughter takes flight.
A whimsical chuckle in the darkest of places,
Where friendships are forged and joy interlaces.

The Ebb and Flow of Nightly Glimmers

When stars play hide and seek in the sky,
Owls wear spectacles, oh so spry.
The moon trips over its own bright face,
While crickets hum in a rhythmic race.

A fox in a tux skips by with glee,
While fireflies dance like they're on a spree.
Clouds try on hats, all puffy and grand,
As nighttime giggles, oh isn't it grand?

The wind tells jokes, although they're quite breezy,
While shadows lounge, feeling a bit cheesy.
Stars wink and wave, hoping to amuse,
In the comedy act, they can't help but lose.

So here we sit, beneath the sky's show,
Counting the laughs as they ebb and flow.
With night's quirky charm, we find pure delight,
In this stage of mischief, our hearts feel light.

Candlelight Reflections in the Dark

A candle flickers, makes faces so bright,
It dances around in the soft, cozy light.
The shadows have parties, they bounce on the walls,
And giggle at whispers, oh how this enthralls.

A cat in the corner, wearing a crown,
Claims the throne on a pillow, looking quite proud.
With a flick of its tail, it swats at the glow,
Making shadows leap like they're putting on a show.

The tablecloth sways, like it's got a mind,
While crumbs from last dinner seem so well-presigned.
Clattering laughter, the teapot spills tales,
As spoons in the cupboard plan their bold fails.

Each glimmer and giggle, a tale to be spun,
In the candlelight's glow, our evening's begun.
With mischief and mirth, the dark finds its spark,
In this silly dance, we revel till dark.

Dusk's Gentle Adornments

At dusk, the sky dresses up in fine threads,
With pinks and purples, it twirls in its beds.
A squirrel in a scarf scampers by with flair,
Searching for acorns, but it finds a spare.

The trees wear hats made of glossy green leaves,
And the breeze writes poems, twisting and weaves.
An old toad croaks tunes from a lily pad's stage,
While dragonflies giggle, feeling quite sage.

The colors chuckle as they do their parade,
While shadows engage in a playful charade.
Moonbeams sashay, showing off their new style,
And everyone smiles, feeling the night's smile.

As dusk drapes its charm, and the day starts to fade,
We dance with the colors, oh what a cascade!
In this whimsical show, we take part and play,
Creating our laughter, as night steals the day.

Hidden Radiance of the Coming Night

As the sun takes a bow, the stars prepare,
With twinkling eyes, they toss back their hair.
A bashful comet zips by with a grin,
Cheers from the galaxies as the night begins.

The crickets form bands, tune their tiny strings,
While moths don their wings, collecting sweet bling.
Fireflies flash like they're running a race,
While owls hoot jokes, finding their own pace.

The dusk shrouded secrets begin to unveil,
As night gets excited, telling a grand tale.
Hidden in shadows are chuckles galore,
With laughter embroidered in night's soft decor.

So here under starlight, we gather and cheer,
For the mischief and magic the night holds near.
With every bright glimmer, the giggles ignite,
In this playful embrace of the coming night.

The Soft Glow of Dusk's Embrace

As the sun slips, it takes a bow,
The squirrels giggle, saying 'Wow!'
How the clouds dress, pink and bright,
While fireflies prepare for their flight.

Crickets chirp in a symphony,
Bees hum along with glee, you see!
A cat in a hat, quite the sight,
Planning its sneaky evening bite.

The stars peek out, all shy and neat,
In the twilight dance, they skip and greet.
A raccoon dons a fancy vest,
Declaring it's the twilight fest!

So grab a snack, enjoy the view,
Laughing at shadows that pass on through.
The dusk is here, it's time to play,
In this magical moment, let's sway!

Shards of Evening's Splendor

The sky is like a painter's brush,
As colors clash in a crazy rush.
A frog in a tux, takes a grand leap,
Singing a tune, while others peep.

Bats in sunglasses flutter by,
Throwing shade like they own the sky.
A dog barks loud, 'This evening's mine!'
While goldfish dream of a dolphin's spine.

The moon rolls in, on a silver stool,
Winking at stars like an old school fool.
A pizza slice hovers overhead,
May all our cravings be widely fed!

And when the night starts to take hold,
Silly gnomes gather, tales to be told.
Laughter echoes through this crazy night,
As shadows dance in a playful light!

Ethereal Hues of the Fading Day

The sun winks out, it's time to play,
Make way for colors, hip-hip-hooray!
A goldfish ponders diving high,
While a hedgehog dreams of learning to fly.

Violet whispers float on the breeze,
Tickling flowers and buzzing bees.
The sky giggles, it tickles so,
As shadows paint their funny glow.

A raccoon stumbles, trips on its toes,
Painting the scene with comical woes.
While owls hoot in an earnest way,
Sharing secrets of the silly sway.

So come, let's dance in this twilight glow,
With laughter echoing, fast and slow.
The day may fade, but fun's still in sight,
In this twilight realm, we ignite the night!

Glistening Dreams at Nightfall

As night falls gently, dreams take flight,
Balloons of laughter fill the night.
A snail in a tutu, spinning 'round,
Twinkling stars up high, all around.

The moon plays hide and seek with the sun,
While kittens weave webs, thinking it's fun.
A jellybean cloud drips candy rain,
Tickling the toes of a dancing train.

Fireflies hold a disco ball near,
Flashing lights that spread the cheer.
The shadows sway, a comical dance,
As the night invites them, 'Come take a chance!'

So join the fun in this glimmering place,
And wear your socks with a quirky face.
In dreams glistening, let's laugh and play,
For in this night, joy leads the way!

Secrets of the Starry Veil

In the sky, those winking dots,
Gather tales like crafty tots.
One's a prince, the other's a cook,
Stealing moons with a secret nook.

A comet slips, it spills a drink,
Stars dance round, quick as you blink.
Planets gossip, oh what a scene,
Flirting with meteorites, so keen!

Constellations swap their hats,
Sipping stardust, where the fun's at.
They giggle and wiggle, what a delight,
Making wishes, hiding from sight.

Up above, a festival flares,
Laughter spills from cosmic Aires.
With tickles from the Milky Way's trails,
The universe sings, no need for sails.

Radiance Beneath the Night Sky

Under the dark, the sparkles gleam,
Shooting stars plot a wild dream.
A pink moon's in on the joke,
Tickling light like a feathered cloak.

Glow worms play a game of tag,
Winking through grass like a cheeky flag.
Fairy lights flash, 'Look at me!'
While whispers sway the midnight tree.

A dance party with shadows galore,
Everyone twirling, wanting more!
Even the owls hoot in time,
Making the evening feel like a rhyme.

Clouds play hopscotch above our heads,
Casting shapes like mischievous threads.
In this glow, giggles collide,
The night sky's stage, our hearts open wide.

Ethereal Sparklers of the Evening

Beneath the veil of a dusky haze,
Twinkling lights begin their plays.
A snail on a star, dressed fancy,
Hitching rides like a wild chancy!

Fireflies chime their little tunes,
Under the gaze of dreamy moons.
Each glow a wink, a silly sign,
Daring shadows to draw the line.

On the breeze, laughter flies,
While crickets share their clever lies.
A raccoon sneaks snacks from a glint,
In the starlit feast, he won't give a hint!

The night flirts with a gentle breeze,
As secrets tumble with the leaves.
Ethereal sparkles giggle and sway,
In this twilight dream, come laugh and play!

Mystical Shimmers of Dusk

As the sun winks its sleepy eye,
Cuddles of colors toss and fly.
Owls in tuxedos start their spree,
Chasing shadows like a game of spree!

Squirrels sharing tales so tall,
With stories of the big nightfall.
They challenge the stars to a dance,
Spinning round like a daring romance.

The darkness hides a playful line,
As laughter echoes, sweet as wine.
Hedgehogs wear hats, just the right size,
Sipping dewdrops, mischief in their eyes.

The moon laughs, and the dusk shivers,
Lighting up all the midnight rivers.
In this magical, silly, bright world,
Every twinkle brings giggles, unfurled.

A Tapestry of Dusk's Delights

In the evening, squirrels dance,
Chasing shadows, how they prance!
With nuts as crowns, they sport and twirl,
As twilight painted the world in swirl.

Bats zoom by, all in a flap,
While crickets share their evening rap.
A frog in a hat leaps with glee,
Singing songs of jubilee!

The moon yawned wide, a sleepy grin,
As fireflies spun a sparkly spin.
Owl's wearing glasses, snoozes deep,
While raccoons plan their nighttime leap.

So cheer for dusk, our comic friend,
Where nature's oddities never end!
We laugh amidst the stars' soft glow,
In this merry show, anything can flow!

Shimmering Echoes in the Gloam

In the gloaming, shadows play,
A cat with a monocle leads the way.
It stumbles over a hidden shoe,
A grand parade of laughter ensues!

Mice with tiny top hats stride,
As moonbeams cast a gleeful guide.
"Step right up!" a toad calls out,
His karaoke makes us shout!

The trees wave arms like they've lost a bet,
Whispering secrets we shan't forget.
Breezes carry giggles afar,
As night unfolds its wacky bazaar.

So here we frolic till stars align,
In this epic, wobbly design.
For every moment brings a tease,
During twilight's joyful, silly freeze!

Stardust and Silhouettes

Starlit dreams in a playful spin,
A penguin jugging, hey, where to begin?
In quirky costumes, critters unite,
For a midnight ball in the cool moonlight.

The shadows wear polka dots and stripes,
Dancing wildly, full of types.
A hedgehog twirls in sequined care,
While a timid turtle joins the fair.

Chuckles bloom like flowers in zest,
As owls in tuxedos start their quest.
"Life's a party!" they hoot with flair,
Bringing laughter to the midnight air!

The night is young, so let's not wait,
To find humor around every gate.
Each moment a spark in this whimsical show,
As stardust glimmers, and joy starts to flow!

Moonlit Charms and Hidden Dreams

A raccoon with dreams of grand cuisine,
Cooks up pancakes, like nothing I've seen!
With syrup rivers and whipped cream mountains,
He dances with glee, oh what a fountain!

The moon peeks down, an amused audience,
While raccoons stage their own brilliance.
"Just add some glitter!" shouts a wise fox,
Mixing shadows in a whimsical box.

Caterpillars chirp in their tune,
As they dream of flying beneath the moon.
But for now they wiggle, wriggle, and sway,
In a tangled jig of dusk's ballet.

So toast the charms that the nighttime brings,
With hidden dreams and all sorts of flings.
In this playful kingdom, let's laugh till we drop,
For the moon's our stage, and we'll never stop!

The Treasure of Dimming Light

As the sun tucks in for the night,
The squirrels steal jewels, oh what a sight!
They laugh and they prance in the fading glow,
Planning a party, just so you know.

The shadows grow long on the trees' embrace,
While raccoons don hats, what a silly place!
With fireflies twinkling, they dance in line,
Who needs diamonds when sparks are divine?

A rabbit reserves a corner for brew,
While chipmunks trade snacks, yes, that's their cue!
The night sky is ripe for an upside-down world,
Where giggles and snacks are merrily hurled.

So gather your friends in the soft twilight,
Where laughter is gold in the coming night.
For treasures abound in every strange sight,
When laughter is endless, and joy takes flight.

Nightfall's Shimmering Veil

Amidst falling stars that wink and twirl,
The owls kick back with a magical whirl.
They hoot with delight in the dusky air,
Transforming the night into their wild fair.

The shadows don hats, as the crickets sing,
While dogs with sunglasses proclaim themselves king.
A bustling parade of nocturnal fun,
Who knew the night could be so well done?

Under the moon's gleam, the rabbit's got moves,
While fireflies flirt, oh, how each one grooves!
With a symphony strange, and snacks on the side,
Let's toast to the night, and go for a ride!

So, chuckle along with the creatures who play,
In the shimmering veil where silliness stays.
For laughter lingers as the worlds start to blend,
In the magic of night, where all lose and mend.

Pearls of the Setting Sun

Watch the sun drop like a clumsy ballerina,
While pigeons hold court, each claiming a fena.
They strut and they skip on their regal path,
In a world full of gems, there's lots of good math.

The stars take their seats, it's a crowded show,
While squirrels crack jokes that only they know.
With laughter like bubbles that float in the air,
They toast to the night without worry or care.

The rabbits debate whether to hop or to nap,
While the raccoons plan heists and take a quick lap.
And just when you think that the dusk feels so tame,
A skunk in a tux jumps into the game!

So here's to the chaos that twilight bestows,
With laughter and antics that nobody knows.
For in this grand evening, each creature's a star,
Making pearls out of functions, not all that bizarre.

Glints of Nocturnal Grace

As shadows creep in like a shy little cat,
The hedgehogs roll dice, who'll win, how 'bout that?
A party erupts in the softening light,
With comets that glimmer and giggles ignite.

The owls wear glasses, looking quite wise,
While fireflies dance, with glints in their eyes.
The wind tells a tale with a cheeky little breeze,
That twists through the trees, causing laughter, if you please!

The garden is buzzing with secrets galore,
As nighttime unfurls, it becomes quite the chore.
A skunk tells a story of an epic close call,
While the raccoons throw popcorn, oh what a brawl!

So linger a moment in this twilight chase,
As joy fills the air, it's just pure embrace.
For what is a night full of funny little dreams,
But glints of pure joy in a world bursting at the seams?

Fragments of Light in Twilight's Arms

In the sky, a wink of gold,
A squirrel's antics, bold and bold.
He juggles nuts, a clumsy feat,
Under the twilight's soft retreat.

A cat joins in, with a purring bounce,
Chasing shadows, it seems to flounce.
With paws like plush, it makes a dash,
While fireflies join in for a flash.

The moon peeks out, a mischievous grin,
As bugs do a dance on a whimsy spin.
A frog croaks tunes, absurdly loud,
The night is silly, and we're proud!

So gather 'round, the twilight's cheer,
With laughter and light, let's make it clear.
In this odd hour, where dreams collide,
We'll chase the quirks that stars provide.

Night's Treasure Trove of Radiance

Hiding in shadows, the glowbugs play,
Mistaking my shoe for a landing bay.
With each little buzz, they bring a chuckle,
As I trip and fall, a nighttime shuffle.

The owls sit wise, but I hear them lough,
Watching my antics, a feathery sloth.
Their eyes roll back as I try to impress,
Swapping bright tales in this nightly mess.

A raccoon sneaks in, planning a feast,
Raiding my picnic, oh what a beast!
With removed sandwich and chips mislaid,
It giggles and scrambles, a raccoon parade!

So raise a glass to the night's silly spree,
Where laughter sparkles, wild and free.
In this treasure trove of silly delight,
We'll dance with the stars, into the night.

The Subtle Glow of Dusk

The sun dips low, a cheeky tease,
Colors splatter like spilled cheese!
A bat zooms by, all quite absurd,
Chasing a bug that just blurred.

The grasshoppers chirp, a late-night song,
While crickets laugh, "We'll join along!"
A butterfly gets caught in a breeze,
Waltzing around like it owns the trees.

A sleepy dog yawns, then miscalculates,
Tripping over its dreams, oh how it states!
With snorts and snores that echo wide,
The twilight giggles, joyfully tied.

So raise a cheer to this gentle phase,
Even in folly, twilight stays.
With whimsy and charm in soft embrace,
Let's greet the night with a silly face.

Celestial Enchantment in Shadows

Under moonbeams, a mouse in a hat,
Dances on whiskers, imagine that!
With tiny taps on a stovepipe drum,
He calls for the stars, and they come!

A turtle trots, like a runaway show,
With a swagger that says, "Here I go!"
Chasing after dreams that glow like jewels,
In this odd realm, we break all the rules.

With laughter that sparkles, oh what a sight,
As shadows play games, in the fading light.
A rabbit dashes with vigor and glee,
As if the night is made just for me!

So here we twirl in this charming glow,
With friends and laughter, a delightful flow.
In the embrace of night, let's take a chance,
For every shadow, holds a dance.

The Dance of Dusk and Diamonds

In the sky, the stars take stage,
Wobbling like a drunk old sage.
They twinkle, stumble, laughing loud,
As day's curtain falls, we're awed and proud.

The moon joins in, a silly sight,
With a smile that's too big, oh what a light!
It winks at clouds, a cheeky tease,
While fireflies dance with boisterous ease.

Night's creatures form a jolly band,
Crickets chirp with a clumsy hand.
They serenade the world anew,
With offbeat rhythms and laughter too.

As stars throw a party, we can't but sigh,
Who knew the night could be such a high?
So grab your friends, let's cheer and play,
In the cosmic dance that ends the day!

Stardust Aglow at Twilight's Edge

At dusk's arrival, the giggles start,
Twinkling orbs do a wobbly part.
They flare and flicker, whoops and grins,
Making mischief as night begins.

A comet zooms with a raucous cheer,
"Who needs sleep? Let's bring in the cheer!"
While meteors race, in a silly parade,
Across the sky, watch their antics played.

The constellations swap their names,
"I'm not a bear, I'm a bird with games!"
They swap places with each goofy flash,
As stardust spills, a cosmic splash.

Oh, the night is alive with jest,
Where every glimmer is a tiny quest.
So laugh with the stars, embrace the fun,
In this mad night under the glowing sun!

Midnight's Secret Treasures

In the dark, the squirrels prance,
Searching for a midnight dance,
They wear their acorn hats with pride,
While moonbeam owls take them for a ride.

The shadows giggle, they play peek-a-boo,
As stars drop secrets, just for a few,
A cat's shadow hums a little tune,
Stealing the night like a cartoon raccoon.

Fireflies blink in a game of chase,
While sleepy dogs dream of a wild race,
The grass whispers jokes to the breeze,
As frogs croak laughter beneath the trees.

So if you hear a chuckle at night,
It's just the world having fun in twilight,
A treasure trove of giggles and cheer,
Midnight's secrets are best shared here!

Luminous Whispers of Evening

Whispers ride the evening air,
As crickets croon without a care,
The moon grins at its silver glow,
While shadows argue on who'll steal the show.

A raccoon dons a diamond-studded mask,
Performing acrobatics—what a task!
His partner, a bird, sings off key,
Together they form a comedy spree.

The stars roll their eyes and twinkle bright,
As ants hold a parade in the soft twilight,
A missing shoe becomes a stage,
For the tiny creatures, a grand new age.

So listen closely to the night's decree,
In laughter, there's treasure, come join the spree,
With every giggle, the last rays bend,
Luminous whispers, where fun knows no end!

Starlit Elegance

In elegant gowns of sparkling light,
The stars waltz gracefully, oh, what a sight,
While planets spin in a dizzy delight,
Hosting a party, oh, what a night!

A comet trips and spills its drink,
Nearby saturns giggle and wink,
The Milky Way hosts a dance-off cheer,
With cosmic jokes only comets hear.

Space bugs stutter in their fancy attire,
Breaking into a jig next to a cosmic fire,
While rockets rocket past in a daring run,
In the galaxy, the laughter's never done.

So if you catch a twinkle in your eye,
Remember the party up in the sky,
Starlit elegance in the night's embrace,
Where funny dreams float at a rollicking pace!

Fragments of Dusk's Delight

At dusk, the colors burst alive,
Chirping birds take a playful dive,
With shades of orange and pink in sight,
Nature crackles with giggles tonight.

A wandering breeze makes the flowers sway,
Tickling tulips, they dance and play,
Tailors of dusk stitch laughter anew,
While butterflies glide, donning shades of hue.

The sun winks as it dips down low,
Painting the sky like a show-off pro,
In puddles, the world becomes a mirror,
Reflecting snippets of joy that draw nearer.

So gather the fragments, let laughter ignite,
In the fading light, everything feels right,
Dusk's delight is a magical spree,
Where humor blooms like a wildflower tree!

Night's Embrace of Shining Dreams

In shadows where giggles bloom,
Laughter dances, dispelling gloom.
Stars wink down with mischievous glee,
Whispers of night, wild and free.

Pajamas on, we prance in delight,
Building castles of dreams in the night.
A sock puppet claims it's a king,
In our world, laughter's the real thing.

We ride unicorns made of cheese,
Dining on sandwiches filled with peas.
The moon's our spotlight, the stage is set,
For silly antics we won't forget.

As bedtime beckons, the giggles fade,
Yet memories linger in the charade.
In dreams, we'll race the stars above,
In this twilight, we find our love.

Embraced in Twilight's Caress

Twilight paints the world with cheer,
As giggling fairies whisper near.
A silly dance in the fading light,
Spinning round till we take flight.

Fireflies join in the fun parade,
Dragonflies bob in the evening shade.
A frog in a top hat leaps in style,
Winking at us with a greeny smile.

Clouds become popcorn in the sky,
As we munch on dreams that flutter by.
A giggle shared with the passing breeze,
In this twilight, our hearts find ease.

With every laugh, the darkness shrinks,
Silly thoughts drifting like shiny blinks.
In moonlit games, we disappear,
Where laughter and joy forever adhere.

Light Unfurled in the Shadow's Hold

At dusk, the shadows start to play,
As goofy goblins join the fray.
With wobbly legs, they leap and twirl,
Giving the night a spin and whirl.

The stars drop candy, sweet and bright,
As we gulp giggles, what a sight!
In a blanket fort, we hide so tight,
Telling tales of monsters that bite.

But wait! They're just marshmallows in disguise,
With squishy bodies and chocolate eyes.
We toast to bravery, though we're a mess,
In this shadow dance, we're truly blessed.

With night in tow, we chase the moon,
Footloose and fancy, to our own tune.
As dawn approaches, we hug the light,
In laughter's embrace, all feels right.

Moments Wrapped in Evening's Brilliance

Evening wraps us in its glow,
With floppy hats and a silly show.
We twirl like dervishes, heartbeats racing,
In this playful dusk, we're forever chasing.

Bouncing shadows on the grass,
Each time a giggle, we let it pass.
Chasing life like it's a breeze,
Finding joy in the little tease.

A cricket sings a comedic tune,
Crashing our party like a balloon.
We laugh till we roll, gasping for air,
Our hearts light as feathers, free from care.

As night whispers secrets with winks,
We gather memories like precious trinks.
In this time of fun, let spirits lift,
Wrapped in laughter, the perfect gift.

www.ingramcontent.com/pod-product-compliance
Lightning Source LLC
Chambersburg PA
CBHW060143230426
43661CB00003B/552